JUST LIVING

This book is the winner of the 2019 Catamaran Poetry Prize for West Coast poets. The Catamaran Poetry Prize is open to all West Coast poets living in the states of California, Alaska, Hawaii, Oregon, and Washington. The prize is open to submissions from November to March.

The judge for the 2019 Catamaran Poetry Prize was **Zack Rogow**, *Catamaran* contributing editor. He is the author, editor, or translator of more than twenty books or plays. His most recent book of poems, *Irreverent Litanies*, was published by Regal House.

JUST LIVING

Susan Browne

Published by Catamaran
1050 River St. #118
Santa Cruz, California 95060

www.catamaranliteraryreader.com

All rights reserved.

Published in the United States of America
Copyright © Susan Browne, 2019

Printed in Shanghai by KS Printing

Designed by Alvaro Villanueva / bookishdesign.com

ISBN: 978-0-578-57380-9

Without limiting the rights under copyright reserved above, no part of this publication (except in the case of brief quotations embodied in critical articles or reviews) may be reproduced, stored in or introduced into a retrieval system, or transmitted, in any form or by any means (electronic, mechanical, photocopying, recording or otherwise), without the prior written consent of both the copyright owner and the above publisher of this book.

COVER ART:
Louise LeBourgeois
Passage, 2017
Oil on panel, 42 x 84 in

FLAPS AND BACK COVER:
Louise LeBourgeois
In the Swells, 2018
Oil on panel, 12 x 12 in

FRONT INSIDE FLAP:
Anda Dubinskis
Idle Afternoon, 2007
Gouache on printed paper, 22 x 30 in

BACK INSIDE FLAP:
Anda Dubinskis
Casa Dami, 2007
Gouache on wrapping paper, 19 x 14 in

for Maureen Baumgartner

Contents

I

Augury	12
Beast	13
Strange Ode	14
Dare	16
Critical Thinking	17
Variation on Texts by Vallejo, Donald Justice, and Patrick Phillips	18
What a Wonderful World	19
Last Night in Sweden	21
Semicolon	23
This Friday	24
Valentine	25
Chiaroscuro	26
Faith is a Thing with Running Shoes	27
Taking It for a Spin	28
Blunder	29
Knife	30

II

Prayer	32
Looking for SoHo in SoHo	33
Home	34
Hurt	35
Adventure	36
Just Living	37
Reprieve	38
After	39
Mountain View Cemetery	40
Summer, 1967	41
Self-Portrait with Mustang & Baby	43
Aubade Ending in Elegy	44
October Violin	46

III

A Brief History of My Life	48
Love Letter	49
Seashell	50
Bloodline	51
Smart TV	53
Black Friday	54
Flamenco	55
Hot as Hell	56
Great	57
Ms. Scrooge	58
Auld Lang Syne	59
While Playing Tennis I Never Think of Death	60
Tremolo	62
In the Wine Country	63
Shepherd Canyon	64
Mandolin Sky	65

I

Augury

I can't get enough of the clouds
and what they do, living side by side.
I can hardly believe we still have weather.
Today, this headline:
Places to Visit Before They Disappear.
Some billionaire will build a wall
around one of those doomed venues and sink
a dozen underground bunkers adorned
with gold and marble fixtures. At the gym,
I walked by a TV as big as the house
I grew up in, and Arnold Schwarzenegger
shot a grenade launcher in my face,
saying, "I've been vaiting for you."
And he's the good guy. Instead of watching TV,
I watch weather patterns. The past
three years, the cherry tree blossomed earlier
and earlier. Today, I sat down on the carpet
of scattered petals and tried to cast
a magic spell, a rising up of a great change
of heart arriving westerly on the global wind.
The first kamikazes painted cherry blossoms
on the sides of their bombers. I sigh a lot now
as if I can't get enough breath. I read
the sky, hoping not to see the flash.
Today, I found hummingbird feathers,
but not the hummingbird.

Beast

On the freeway at night,
so many car lights, a sea of crawling lamps,
how could there be even one more car
inching in from the snarl
of ramps? We'll make room until there's no more
room, and that seems now but around the bend more
cars while NPR says there isn't enough ice anymore
so the polar bears starve. We know the list
of coming extinctions. We don't discuss this
starving or the twelve million children
who go to bed hungry in America. We're on our way
to dinner. Two hours to drive twenty miles, and we're afraid
of running out of gas. Finally at the restaurant,
we have to park a mile away and slink
among abandoned dogs through dark streets,
let's go over here no there watch out that's a person,
the homeless camped on the sidewalk, litter rolling
in the ashy wind, thousands of acres on fire up north
and down south, making a Spare the Air day,
week, year. We wait an hour for a seat at
the bar—there isn't room in the restaurant
until 10:00 p.m., when it closes. We're so hungry
we aren't hungry. What did we want?
An amber wave of grain. A fruited plain.

Strange Ode

I wanted love so badly
I flew to Cedar Rapids
to stay with a man I barely knew,

and when I arrived at his house,
we chatted for a bit, and he poured
us each a glass of wine and after

a few sips asked if I'd pee
on his head. He was a psychologist,
so I hoped he was joking.

We'd met in a bar in San Francisco—
I was often in a bar in those days,
as if love lived there.

My father was an alcoholic
and my mother had just died,
and looking back at who I was then,

I realize I was crazy from grief.
But at the time I didn't know what
I was doing and a stranger had asked

a strange question. "In the kitchen?"
I asked, because that's where we were,
my small suitcase next to the chair.

"No," the man said. "In the shower."
I glanced into the living room: dark wood floor,
dark furniture, drapes closed in midafternoon.

Fear zithered my rib cage. I hadn't told anyone
where I was. This man could kill me and bury me
in his backyard, and no one would ever find out.

"I think you'd enjoy it," he said.
"And if you'd like me to, I can also pee
on your head." "No, thanks."

I chuckled, but it sounded
like a chicken bone
was stabbing my larynx.

We went for a drive through a beautiful forest
by a river to his parents' house. The father
wore a blue seersucker suit, and the mother's dress

was patterned with peonies. His parents
were so kind I felt like I was their daughter.
When they asked about my family,

I said my mother had died in a car accident,
and while I cried, no one said anything
until I was able to stop. The mother held

my hand the whole time. After dinner,
her son and I sat in the backyard
eating ice cream.

I'd never seen fireflies before.
They made a gold constellation
like a sky of stars beneath the stars.

When we got back to his place, we put on
our pajamas and went to bed. He held me
close and told stories from his childhood.

"Shower?" he asked.
I said the fireflies were good enough.
In the morning, I decided to go home,

so he changed the ticket. At the airport,
he gave me a wrapped present, saying it
was something for my journey. As the plane

lifted off, I opened the package, a book:
You Can Be Happy No Matter What
and I couldn't put it down.

Dare

desolate & determined
spent your twenties marrying & divorcing
trying to be what   it was hopeless   every spring
another busted heart   oh more yes
than molly bloom could imagine   you wanted to experiment
a woman's life sucked   why shouldn't you   like it new
like it nude with your boots on
in the snow   on the swing
in a hot middle of a night   don't forget the museum
& the pumpkin patch of screaming crows   on the ping-pong table
after you beat him   you beat him good   & why shouldn't you
you were just as good or better   you were better   the letter
said he'd never speak your name again   how dare you
decline marriage number three   you had steel inside he said
you thought a little steel was fine   living alone when women didn't
how dare you live alone   how many times did you hear
do you have children   a woman not having children
or dreaming of curtains couches crock-pots   what a shame
the magic in being
without someone's idea of you   a kind of splendor
traveling through loneliness   its temples & alleys
like rising at dawn each morning
to run silent streets   the loyal sound of one breath
after another & coming home glittered with sweat or rain
letting faith begin the days
if not end them   candles lit   flowers in a vase
a simple warm meal   always a song
crying for all the reasons

Critical Thinking

Today my Iranian student tells me about his sister,
hanged in her office for her political writings,
and he says he has no hope for the world regardless
of what he's learned in my Critical Thinking class,
though he enjoyed the books we read
and the film about the life of Buddha.

My student from Afghanistan apologizes
for the length of her six-page essay
about her brother, beaten to death
in Germany by neo-Nazis.
Then I drive and think about retiring.
In the traffic before the tunnel,
a lowrider screeches past, zaps back in line,
music booming, and something is tied
to the bumper—a stuffed toy, donkey or dog?
The soft thing scrapes along, smacking again
and again against the concrete, and I think
of my student's description of the knuckle
impressions in her brother's *bluish-black* chest
and of the Taliban cutting off the heads
of disobedient women and leaving
their bodies in the soccer stadium.

As I make the last turn toward home,
past dark waves of mountain, the sky's
silver beach, wild beauty not ruined yet,
I think of my quiet student from China
who asked if I was enlightened, and I said,
"Not even close." He seemed so disappointed
that when we left the classroom and stood
in the rain while sunlight moved from behind
the clouds, I said, "Maybe now,"
and we walked to the parking lot,
leaning close together under his umbrella.

Variation on Texts by Vallejo, Donald Justice, and Patrick Phillips

No one will die in my backyard
In the sun on a day in May
When the wind polishes the roses
And the wings of the bees.

It will be a Saturday like today,
A day without elegy,
When my heart is not keening,
When my friends join me at the table
For wine and laughter.

No one is dead.
In May, in my backyard, on a Saturday,
There will be a party,
And nothing is wrong in our bodies,
And we are not alone.

Even when the rain comes,
We let the drops dazzle
In our hair, and no one drives away
Along the darkening road.

We stay together
Under the patio umbrella
For more stories and song,
And never before did life seem so full,
And the gravediggers rest their shovels,
And, out of respect, take a swig from their flasks.

What a Wonderful World

After I drive away,
leaving him at the assisted living home,
I pull over to the side of the road
and watch tumbleweeds rolling
across a field of rocks.

At lunch, my father wanted to know
why he's still alive.

Possible answers:

    1. To learn more
    2. Bad luck
    3. Stubborn heart

He's asked me this for decades,
he's asked me since my mother died
in a car wreck, but even as a teenager,
I worried about his interest in living.

He has never stopped chasing Rommel across the desert.

Wing tips, neckties, briefcases.
Martini lunches the only reprieve.
Rehabs, ERs, fire trucks.

Searching for him
when he'd go on a bender, finding him
sitting on the couch, his face a mask of dried blood,
his eyes unblinking as I stepped over
the vodka bottles and he said, "The bottles won."

The psych ward after I fifty-one-fiftied him,
the detoxing on a gurney, shaking, staring
at me from way down, working hard
to pull himself up.

His miraculous years sober
before he disappeared again

to show up at Dino's drinking coffee,
quiet and sad, surrounded by velvet
paintings of Emmett Kelly.

I start the car and turn on the stereo.
If there are tears,
they are part of the tumbling.
Are we polished enough?
The song is one I've heard
so many times before.

Living long ago by the sea, Father.
I was your Lupine. Your blue flower.

Last Night in Sweden

"You look at what's happening," he told his supporters. "We've got to keep our country safe. You look at what's happening in Germany, you look at what's happening last night in Sweden. Sweden, who would believe this?" Not the Swedes. Nothing particularly nefarious happened in Sweden on Friday.
—Sewell Chan, "'Last Night in Sweden'? Trump's Remark Baffles a Nation," *New York Times*, February 19, 2017

Last night in Sweden
something very bad happened.

People, and immigrants, too,
were sleeping.

Something very bad happened
last night in Sweden.

Before sleeping people,
and refugees, too,

ate meatballs.
Look at all those immigrants,

and refugees, too,
shopping at IKEA

before eating meatballs
and sleeping

last night in Sweden.
Something very bad happened.

There are so many problems.
Who would believe it?

Look at what's happening
in Sweden. Last night

people all over the place,
and refugees everywhere

and immigrants, too, sleeping
in IKEA in large numbers

and eating all the meatballs.

Semicolon

Today is a riot of petals,
cherry-blossom blizzard, eighty-one degrees
in February. I teach the subtleties
of the semicolon and try not to sadden
for my student who's writing about
her leukemia. She told me there's no
match for her marrow, the meds
make her fat and soon she'll be
immune. She wants to learn more
about punctuation, and I wish I had more
to offer than a period on top
of a comma, something bone-deep.
NASA says an asteroid the size
of two football fields could hit Earth.
The odds are one in a quarter million.
What's odder than that?
Being alive. We must never be immune
to each other. After class, we walk
among crushed flowers, and I pause
and see her eyes are the color of violets.

This Friday

Often I wonder what happened
to lost buttons as well as husbands.
We are in love and then not and then
our coats hang open.

You can't think too much about who you are
because you're not that person.
You're more like a lamp. On, off. On, off.

The light on my hands looks real,
and so does my skin with its gold hairs
like any soft animal's.
The body is a museum of trinkets
and hatchets and unsent letters.

I'm concerned about coffins.
There are many of them
disrupting the moss.

What if you could snap
your fingers and disappear?
What if you couldn't snap
yourself back? It would be okay
during committee meetings
when I hear the word *productivity*.

This Friday, my father will be eighty-seven.
He wants socks and spaghetti.

You and I both know the trouble we've seen.
Here, let me button your coat.

Valentine

I once walked past a man on February 14
who was peeing on a window display,
teetering on his tiptoes & bent backward,
aiming at the word *love* written in red curlicues.
Robins fat as cupids watched from the hedges.
At the end of the block I had to look again, too.
He was still going at it like an acrobat or a camel.
I thought I might do the same thing
if I had the equipment because love was a spike
in the vena cava or an arrow in the brain,
the great spurns of fate turning kisses into thorns.
Sometimes I make myself sick with nostalgia.
I can't help it if I listen to Dan Fogelberg radio.
I used to play Dan's song "Longer" on the guitar
& weep that my longest relationship was with my dog.
She once pulled the sock out of a man's shoe
while he was wearing it in my doorway.
My dog didn't stop growling for an hour
after he left. She knew he wasn't for me,
but who was? & then I met you.
We once kissed all day long & lost weight.
My students all got As, called themselves the Love Class.
I once told you that in my next life I'd be a weatherperson
& asked what you'd be. "Dead," you said.
If my dog had still been alive then,
she'd have known you were the guy for me.
Even though we've been together longer
than any forest primeval, I want to go to bed with you
in this dark middle of an afternoon,
tell you about the cumulonimbus & nimbostratus clouds
that mean rain is on its way. Without any words,
let me teach you the word *petrichor*, which means
that earthy smell that accompanies first rain
after a long spell of warm, dry weather.

Chiaroscuro

The Italian birds fly over the garden
where this morning I stood on sunstruck
tiles next to an olive orchard,
thinking how fortunate to land here,
eating the earth, drinking the vineyard,
traveling to Rome to a room of Caravaggios
that nearly stop me from breathing,
especially the painting where Mary,
her skin incandescent, leans out of the gloom
to help her young son try to crush the snake's head,
his little luminous foot on top of his mother's,
the details eerie and real as if I could touch each figure
and feel the plush of flesh, as if the serpent
could uncoil and slither out of the frame.
Later, in the taxi, the driver tells me about
the shooting—a nightclub in Florida—
and then I'm back in the garden,
mumbling a prayer although it's only us
who can save us, as I watch the birds cross
the sky, sweeping the light into their dark wings.

Faith Is a Thing with Running Shoes

Scrolling down my iPhone calendar, I stop at 2071.
That year, my birthday is on a Sunday. I'll be 119.
If I had to add it all up, I'd say I was way too normal.
I can't believe I spent a minute feeling guilty
for having lots of boyfriends in my youth
or having sex with two men in one day. It wasn't easy
getting from the east side of town to the west side
on my bicycle in time. I should keep the faith.
Yesterday, I was in a hot tub with two men.
They were discussing earthquake preparedness.
One said he had a kit that could filter
any kind of water, including sewage.
The other said he had a rafter built in his garage
to protect his car, and it could support
the local high school cheerleading squad doing pull-ups.
Or so the builder had advertised. I have nothing prepared
for an emergency, except a gallon of Tanqueray
in the cupboard above the oven because I gave up gin
after my second divorce. Maybe this means I have faith
in something. At least twice a week I wake up astonished
at how living calmly goes on, shoulder to shoulder
with unreckonable tragedy. The men paused
to take a scrolling glance when I stepped out of the hot tub.
Then they went on about where to store the food
and the importance of keeping a pair of running shoes
under the desk at the office.

Taking It for a Spin

What I loved about my Barbie Doll
was her car, a red convertible
she drove all over town.
She didn't trust Ken's driving
but sometimes invited him along.
Sometimes she got out of the car
and walked with Ken into the pasture
behind the living room chair and laid
herself on top of him. This occurred soon after
the invention of Creedence Clearwater Revival.
My Barbie wasn't born on the bayou,
but she wasn't afraid of chasing down a hoodoo,
and she was never going to get stuck in Lodi again.
She broke up with Ken, she broke up with a lot of Kens.
They were exactly the same, totally plastic,
wanting her to spend more time
at her Barbie Glam Vanity Set than in her car.
My Barbie wanted to go to England, to college
in Cambridge. She would go everywhere
and learn everything about what
a woman can do. She couldn't imagine
not being able to vote or own property
or having as many rights as cattle.
The kind of cow with a tag in her ear.
Some people in America still think a woman
should be tagged. My Barbie will, in due time,
drive to Washington, DC, and park in the Oval Office.
She will take the Dems and the GOP out for a spin
toward a new vision. My Barbie knows for sure,
just like you do, the future belongs to her.

Blunder

I called Lorna Lorena
and Lorna was upset
because she doesn't like Lorena
for something Lorena did. I never got the full
story, we started playing tennis, and while
we hit I was deep in my head—
you know how far you can go
in that sphere of dimensionlessness—
and without realizing it, I called Lorna Lorena
again. "Don't ever call me that name!" she yelled.
I apologized and at the break went into the restroom
and repeated, "Lorna, Lorna, Lorna,"
but kept thinking *Lorena*.
You know how hard it can be to control what you want
to control, some kind of inner prankster jangling
your chain like a Lorenic Tourette's.
Later on, Lorna made a great shot,
and I said, "Great shot, L . . . L . . . L . . . Lorna."
She stared at me like I'd turned into Lorena.
That stare was so thorough, I wasn't sure I wasn't Lorena.
I decided not to use anyone's name
for the rest of the day, and I shouldn't be
using Lorna's name now because if she ever
sees it, I'll wish to God I were someone else.
Maybe my neighbor Laura, who's on vacation
trekking the Road to Nowhere in Iqaluit, Nunavut.
In important ways we are everyone else.
And there are times when I want to change
my name. I think of Rocky Balboa,
that bloody scene in the ring when he cries out
"AAADRIIAANNN!"
after he's lost the fight. What a beautiful sound
when love beats everything.

Knife

I run on the path at the same time each day
When there are others on the path so I'm not alone
Because a woman shouldn't run alone,
Not without mace or a knife
Or a dog trained to kill.
The varieties of violence are endless,
Like the guy who sits on a bench, saying, "Come on, honey,
Pick up the pace!" Or, "Yawanna win this race?"
Or, "Good girl!"
I've heard it all from men licking their lips,
From men standing in my way
Offering their demands and drivel.
I don't want to swagger over to the man,
To a city of men, a country of men
And push them down
And slice my knife through their pants
And lift up their dicks with my blade
And say, "Not bad!"
I don't want revenge or to hate
Like I hated the men
Who tried to rape me—the man at the party
And the man in the hills—
The too-many men who want me to believe
I'm as worthless as the body they could hurt.
When this man on the bench whistles
And claps like I'm his personal showgirl,
I keep running on my muscled legs,
My will forged in a crucible
To a very fine point, honed by the women
Before me, and the women after,
Sharper and sharper,
Who know exactly what they want,
Who grow stronger and stronger at a rapid pace,
Who will slit these men from crotch to sternum.

Prayer

Dear Lord, when I was ten I started to question you
& turned to rocks.
They came from Secret Creek.
That's what I called the dark gully behind my house
where what seemed like a thousand birds sang at once.
I stored my rocks in a shoebox lined with velvet.
Quartz was my favorite because of its magnificent glow,
so I kept it on my nightstand & put away my Virgin Mary lamp.
Dear Lord, I have believed in a rabbit's foot, tarot cards,
the *I Ching*, & a Magic 8 Ball.
Also Phyllis Diller & Camus.
& you again, dear Lord, then didn't then did, & it goes on
like that, like a sacred Möbius strip or a Heraclitean yo-yo.
Dear Lord, my friend has new tumors in her stomach.
She almost died trying to kill the first tumors
with surgery & chemo, & it worked then didn't.
Dear Lord, sometimes I think tears are God.
Not self-pitying tears but tears from Secret Creek.
Dear Lord, I appreciate living. I stop & smell the wisteria.
Dear Lord, you did a good job with the wisteria.
Dear Lord, my friend is a singer, she sang for you.
She rubbed talcum powder into her thighs,
under her nylons, because she sweat on stage.
Dear Lord, some talc contains asbestos. Mothers rubbed it on their babies.
Dear Lord, lots of times we don't know what we're doing.
Forgive me, but is it the same for you?
Dear Lord, I'm concerned, overall, about your holy purposes:
demagogues & nuclear codes, for example.
Dying, Jesus sweat great drops of blood.
Camus said, *Live to the point of tears*,
but couldn't we be tender without so much pain?
Lord, dear God, have mercy.

Looking for SoHo in SoHo

Many streets, but not the streets
we wanted, and many shops,
but not the shops we wanted. We wanted
a different place, not where we were,
although we swore we'd been there before
and thought it was near,
so we kept on, and finally
we asked someone where it was, and she said,
Where you are, but we didn't believe it.
Where the cobblestones, where the leafy trees
with branches like filigree,
where the little shops crammed with curios?
We were thirsty, exhausted, asking
each other where, where did it go?
If we found it, we could rest, it would be
the destination, the answer to our question,
a question of meaning, of rescue
from other places, streets, shops, meanings
that hadn't done their job to soothe our seeking.
Now it was evening, but we continued,
turning corners and decades, growing old,
dying, dead, yet persevering, reincarnating,
searching through centuries for that one
small street, cool, quiet, except for the *tap-tap*
of our shoes entering where we'd find
what had been hidden from us
all of our lives, our many, many lives.

Home

For years I lived in basement apartments.
One had a mud floor in the closet, another didn't

have a stove. The rare cooking that took place
occurred in the toaster. The family upstairs

was always doing laundry, so I ate
my toasted pancakes and listened

to the spin cycle and looked out
my porthole window as I churned along.

Occasionally, a sort of boyfriend sailed by
with wilted roses, the discount tag still glued

to the cellophane, in gratitude for the expensive
dinner I'd bought him because

he'd forgotten his wallet again, and because
I'd helped him realize he really did want to be

a monk. What happened everywhere I went
was exactly the same, even if he parted

his hair on the left instead of the right.
Then I rented a studio on top of a house

on top of a hill, one wall of the living room
a sliding glass door. Most nights I left it open

to the North Star, to the clang of the buoy,
to the city below, its acres of lighted windows

burning with destinies and why not love my own?
Meanwhile, six thousand miles away,

he who would be my home started packing.

Hurt

Cleaning the lint out of the dryer screen
and shoving it back into its slot,
I cut my arm on the sharp corner,
a gash from wrist to almost elbow,
and watched the skin redden, the flesh open,
the blood flow out and wondered
in a shocked sort of haze if maybe
I should drive to Emergency or was I going
to faint, staring at the crimson
splotching the laundry room floor;
I slathered on ointment and wrapped
a dish towel around my arm and sat down
to wait for the bleeding to stop, while
I remembered past hurts and the invisible
lacerations and traumas, and how in less
than a second things can change
irrevocably, and I thought of my friend
who said she believed in reincarnation
because of her dreams, but this time
she was spinning off the wheel of life and death,
and she was glad, and I asked if her life
was that bad, and she said no, her life
was perfect, smiling her mystic smile
that in my heart she's famous for,
but I would miss her in my next turn
around the gyre, and I unwrapped the towel
and pretended to be brave and placed
ten Band-Aids up my arm and carried on
with the day, going out into the yard to gawk
at the sudden explosion of pink rose
blossoms, each the size of my fist, opening.

Adventure

You decided to skydive
to face your fear of heights.
I thought it a great adventure
and wore your big camera
around my neck so I could take photos
of you floating in Pacific skies.
But then I saw the dinky blink of a plane,
and you, an infinitesimal dot
plummeting through the overwhelming blue.

I raced up and down the beach,
your camera banging against my chest,
my heart falling with you,
tears flying out of my eyes.
I crashed onto my knees. You were still a dot,
becoming a speck with arms, then legs,
and you must have pulled the cord,
while I must have blacked out for a minute,
because you were on the ground—
your bones unsmashed—
grinning like a maniac.
I shook like your parachute
whipping in the wind.

We'd been together a few years,
and okay I thought I loved you,
but not like this, what was this?
Like standing on the edge of a cliff,
the breathtaking view, wolf spiders
hidden among the poppies.

At the bar for margaritas,
you said, "*Salud*," and I couldn't speak.
Your body returned from the ether,
your face reassembled from mist.

Just Living

I didn't have time to masturbate this morning. It's right there at the top of my to-do list, but I have way too many things to do. I'm retired and busier than ever. I started meditating every morning, so now I don't know which to do first: meditate or masturbate. Probably makes more sense to masturbate and then meditate because I would be more relaxed, but sometimes masturbating can take a while, depending, so I might have to skip meditation and then feel lousy that I didn't get everything done. I could alternate, I guess. Masturbate on Mondays and meditate on Tuesdays and so forth. Skip Wednesdays because my husband and I usually have sex on Wednesdays, the whole point of the daily masturbation program. My doctor prescribed masturbation. "Do it as much as possible," she said. The old use it or lose it. After I told my doc how much time it was taking out of my day, she recommended using a vibrator to speed things up. We went online to look at choices—she was surprised I didn't have a vibrator—and then I remembered the one my friend had given me for my birthday a long time ago. It was small, a Sunbeam; I think that was the brand name. My friend had called it a "traveler" because it was so portable. You could put it in your purse or your coat pocket and use it anytime anywhere. Well, almost anywhere. I wouldn't use it, say, in Costco, although I could, easily; just duck behind the gargantuan mountain of megarolls of paper towels, or better yet, behind the floor-to-ceiling stacked boxes of Cuervo tequila. I could break open a bottle, take a few chugs, turn on the traveler, and ¡Ándale! I'm starting to get ideas: put on my headphones and listen to my meditation while shopping at Costco and then cruise with my traveler for a quickie and a brief happy hour. Thinking further, masturbation really is a kind of meditation. Ergo, is meditation a kind of masturbation? I miss teaching my Critical Thinking class. I bet my students would have a rousing discussion on this topic. I went home from the doc's and searched the closets for my little Sunbeam. Then I got sidetracked with throwing stuff away. My husband asked me what I was looking for, and when I told him, he said, "Oh." We aren't big fans of electronics in bed. I even have a problem with using an electric toothbrush. I don't mean for masturbation, I mean for my teeth. It rattles my brain or something. I'm not in favor of electric or battery-operated gizmos around my orifices. My husband isn't crazy about vibrators, either. He thinks he should be enough, that he's better than a machine. But these are desperate times, and we discussed it, and he understands. After all, it's doctor's orders. When I finally found the traveler, I turned it on, and it needed batteries. I wrote *Go to Costco* on my to-do list. I might try out my new plan with the headphones, et al. Cleaning took hours, so multitasking is a must to catch up. I wouldn't exactly say I'm retired. Just living takes a lot of work.

Reprieve

for Kerry

Firemen cut my sister from a car,
pulled her through the shattered back window.
One held her head so she wouldn't move,
so the Jaws of Life wouldn't saw her in half.
She held so still, listening to the keening
of metal, then a river of quiet and she was back
to watch our mother being helicoptered
to the hospital for no reprieve.

My sister and I hike along the flume,
and I can see the scar on her leg
from the gash that glittered with shards of glass—
it had taken the ER nurse hours
to tweeze them out. As we walk,
sometimes she takes my hand. Her wrists
are delicate, but she is strong with gratitude,
and I learn it from her palm against mine.
I want to obey her law of optimism,
wear it around my neck like a small cross
on a fine, almost invisible chain.

After

It was after the accident,
after the twelve-hour surgery,
after the coma. *Get Well Soon*

Mylar balloons floated eye level
around the room. The doctor came in.
It was time. They would take her away.

Where? I asked. To the morgue.
Where is that? In the basement.
Told to leave, we didn't leave.

We watched the orderlies
lift her onto a gurney. I don't remember
if they covered her face with a sheet

like in the movies. Then
the room broke into pieces
like dots in a pointillist painting.

I wasn't thinking anything.
Only *Basement.*
Basement.

Somehow I was on the phone
in a white hallway, but I hung up,
unable to say *My mother died.*

Somehow I arrived at her house,
her rosebushes blossoming,
her dog barking at something

I couldn't see. In the kitchen,
her handwriting in the little
squares of the calendar.

Mountain View Cemetery

I've been wanting to spend time here
since TripAdvisor gave it a good review.
Also, I bought a Fitbit recently
and need to get in my ten thousand steps.
The leaves of the trees make a green canopy
above the streets leading to a mountain of tombstones.
Along the way, fields of them.
I like the one that reads *Last Call*
and stop to check my steps at MOTHER
in large letters.
I imagine her thirteen or fourteen children
huddled where I stand, their bonnets and caps,
their scuffed boots with laces.
Further on, I come to grandiose crypts.
From my research I know this is "Millionaires' Row,"
rich and famous folk—politicians, industrialists,
gold rushers, artists. Crocker, Morgan, Ghirardelli, Norris.
And Elizabeth Short, also known as the Black Dahlia.
In a dream a few nights ago, there was a "Changeover Station"
where you get your next life. The dream was matter-of-fact.
For God's sake, if anyone should have another chance, it's Elizabeth.
At the top of the mountain, my Fitbit vibrates.
My steps are halfway completed.
I sit by a rainbow pinwheel that spins like crazy,
the small stone next to it set deep and private in the grass.
The view is spectacular,
stretching out over Oakland to San Francisco Bay.
A few yards away, a young man leans against the statue
of an angel whose huge wings hold the sky in place.
His thick hair ruffles in the breeze.
It kills me.
A couple strolls by, arm in arm, faces lifted to the sun.
We could put our steps together and celebrate,
the mountain only a hill leading down to water.

Summer, 1967
for Cheryl

My sister and I
lay on chaise lounges
by the garbage cans
where the sun was strongest,
reflecting off the white gravel
in the side yard rotisserie,
slicking our bikini bodies
with Wesson oil and holding
a square of aluminum foil
under our chins to catch
the rays and tan our faces
so boys would love us,
marry us, have babies with us,
O, domestic bliss,
which we believed in with all
our sunburned hearts
despite the truth
to the contrary everywhere—
our neighbor Mr. Prescott,
found most Sundays
passed out on his crabgrass,
and Mrs. Rudgear,
wrapped in a straitjacket
and paddy-wagoned away
from the Bridge Club.
We curled our hair or ironed it
and put on makeup,
not too much—we didn't
want to look like sluts,
although we dreamed ceaselessly
about what the sluts were up to
as we curled our eyelashes
and would have ironed them, too,
if we'd thought that would help.
We spent hours, years, a decade
getting dressed, then stood
in the downtown rec center
in a reeking aura of Heaven Scent

between the Ping-Pong tables,
batting our blue-shadowed lids,
waiting for a boy to gangle over,
open his mouth a centimeter,
and say, "Hey."
We thought our smooth skin
would last forever, even though
Bobby Dylan sang,
The times they are a-changin'.

Self-Portrait with Mustang & Baby

while my older sister & her boyfriend lay like a tangy meatloaf
on the good green couch in our parents' living room I took off
with my baby sister in the boyfriend's mustang convertible in search
of pop-tarts & yahtzee scorecards he gave me cash for
to buy more private time to rub the madras off her blouse
I was ecstatic cruising with kerrykins
tied to the passenger seat with a beach towel
shaking her chubby fists to "born to be wild"   at kmart
we got the stash   drove the long way back on tassajara road
rolling hills of horses oaks mustard grass those enormous shiny crows
caw-cawing   we were on the wing until I stopped to change
a diaper have a smoke finding a dented slightly shredded one
in the glove box   on our way again in the feral wind
baby sleepy now her head with its three tufted curls nodding down
to her chest   I wanted to keep going to europe at least idaho but
could we live on pop-tarts & she needed her sun hat   the world
a blue-green dazzle fleeting by too beautiful too repetitive at its domestic
boring core   oh I'd never settle down   there were other choices
available as missing buttons or socks   never believe
I'd be married at nineteen   two years away
right around the bend

Aubade Ending in Elegy

Every morning, we woke up
In the huge bed you made for us
With drawers and shelves where
We kept our clothes and books,
And on Sundays we slept in,
Made love, then read to each other,
All day sometimes, we'd bring
Our lunch back to bed, along with
The dog and the cat and my guitar
And your ashtray and our journals,
Where you'd draw and I'd write
Until dusk when we were hungry
Again and thirsty, and we finally
Got up and put music on
The stereo and drank beer
And danced and played cards,
And if it was cold or raining,
You'd build a fire and I'd bring out
The blankets so we could lie
On the couch and fall asleep
In each other's arms, the dog
By our side on the floor, the cat
At our feet, the record skipping,
Making little clicks because it was over,
And sooner than we could have ever
Imagined, it was over between us,
I moved out, and you moved away,
And I only saw you once,
You were remarried
And had a child,
I saw the toy lamb in the back seat of your car,
How it shocked me, you were someone's father,
How I was supposed to have that life
With you,
And the years passed like fire,
I heard you had died,
The neighbor found you,
Sick from drink for a long time,
And I wanted to go to the funeral

But didn't feel I had the right
Although we were together at the start
Of our adult lives
So I thought I should be there
At the end, I remember the time
I had a fever, and you turned my pillow
Over to cool my cheek, I remember you
Drawing a green heart on my palm
With our names inside.

October Violin

Babies don't give a damn if you dress them up for Halloween.
You're just doing that for yourself, right?
It could be festive to make the babies look like pumpkins
or Draculas, or one baby could be a fiddle and the other a violin.
The babies could be twins, fraternal,
and there's a difference between a violin and a fiddle.
You don't spill beer on a violin.
I'm not saying you should spill beer on a fiddle,
especially if it's a baby. I remember the October when
I rode on a motorcycle through Golden Gate Park
with a boyfriend I was about to break up with,
and I kissed his hair and held him tighter
and wondered as I ached for the beauty
of silver fog and orange leaves falling
if I would always be in love
with melancholy. We drove
to an Irish pub on Clement Street to listen
to the fiddlers. Even then, I could hear a violin
in the distance. And what of the babies?
They drift like ghosts in the fog.

III

A Brief History of My Life

I was conceived in a Motel 6 in Henderson, Nevada,
down the road from an atomic bomb
testing site, during a chain-lightning storm.
Mom was scared, having been nearly fried by a bolt
when she was ten while riding her bike in Paradise,
a mining town formerly known as Poverty Ridge,
famous for buffalo nickels and orange dirt,
but she still managed to roll out from under the bed
and grab Dad, who was shell-shocked from surviving
the massacre at Omaha Beach. They pooled
their resources and hit the jackpot of *moi*,
and shortly thereafter, I pondered Howdy Doody,
concerned about the existential oddness
of breathing, puppetry, and why our pet parrot
kept yelling *Muy borracho!*

I fell in love over and over, most notably with a clown
who didn't mind juggling, but I lost him like a sock
so eloped with a sword-swallower. He didn't last long.
Disconsolate, I invented a perfume, *Destroyed*,
which no one bought. Then I got a job
judging odors, turned loss into a religion,
and settled down to epiphanies.

Sixty-three billion years passed, and for a lot of it
I was dead, but the minute I mused, *Maybe we aren't
evolving or devolving but revolving*, Mom pedaled by,
Dad on the handlebars playing the accordion
and with each press of the bellows,
lightning bolted out of Mom's head.
"What are you doing in Paradise?" she asked.
"Waiting for you," I said.

Love Letter

Mom, you've been gone so long
the Berlin Wall is less than dust.
Two grandchildren you never met
are in college. One of them plays
"Moon River" on the piano like you used to,
and some of your jazz favorites.
There've been ten thousand
appalling and amazing changes
in the world. You'd like it
that women hit serves as fast as men.
I'm on marriage number three,
but it's lasted past the month-to-month
lease, and I live in a house
instead of that remodeled garage
where you cried because
of the dirt floor in the closet.
I'm older than you ever were.
Although I think of you almost daily,
I can't hold a picture of you
in my mind; it fades like a breath print
on glass. Even my long anger
about the way you died is like
a memory of a memory. Your ghost
has never visited, but I've had two dreams
of you: In one we walk along the beach,
and you're dressed in white shorts and T-shirt,
those sandals with the jeweled strap
between your toes. You can't speak
but seem fine, like you're on vacation.
In the other, you lie on the ground,
sleeping. Large doves encircle you
and won't let me in. You are far away now.
Or maybe so close I've been living
for both of us. Out my window, the fog
laced with salt and light lifts from the trees.
I can see the ocean you loved
from here, where I remain yours.

Seashell

Here I am on Mother's Day without a mother.
Here I am on Mother's Day without children.
Here I am on Mother's Day hiding out
so I don't have to watch the mothers
with their children and grandchildren
in the park eating tuna sandwiches
cut diagonally and with the crust sliced off.
That's how my mother used to make
my tuna sandwiches, my peanut butter
and mayo, my cheese and mustard.
She's been gone since I almost can't remember,
and my children have been gone always.
Yes, you can miss what you've never had.
Here I am on Mother's Day asking myself,
What have you done with your life? I ask
myself because there's no one else here.
My husband works on Mother's Day,
cooking for mothers and their children.
I lived. I learned to make my own sandwiches
and eat them cut straight across and even
with the crust if I had to, and I never complained,
except on Mother's Day. Here I am
on Mother's Day, opening the door,
walking into the yard to pick some lavender.
There are bees humming among the lilacs.
There is a cat, and I call, "Fifi, come to Mommy."
Fifi yawns and falls back to sleep in the ivy.
There are decisions made by not making them.
There was the grief I cradled.
The ship I sailed on and always looked back.
Every time I'm at the beach I think it's all
still possible. I was a child there with my mother.

Bloodline

In the TV series I'm addicted to,
one of the main characters, Danny, buys cocaine
& does lines in his truck then walks into a bar

& drinks six shots of tequila. I rewound
the scene so I could count them like I used to
count my father's drinks. Danny slinks into

the bathroom, finishes off the bag of coke,
& returns to the bar to drink more until
he can barely stand up but still manages to lift

his arm to get the shot glass to his mouth although
there's a cigarette where the booze needs to go
so the logistics are complicated. Watching him

is like watching a body being burned alive.
I'm dying for him to drink a large glass of water
& go to bed. "Go to bed, goddamnit goddamnit."

I screamed before I called the cops & they took
my father away. I can see the boy
in Danny's eyes behind the shame & sorrow

that have turned his face into a shattered pane of glass.
He shambles along the highway & into a ratty
backyard where a guy offers him a crack pipe.

"Don't smoke it!" I yell from the couch.
Later, he has a dream, which at first I'm not sure
is a dream. He puts a gun to his head.

"No! No!" I shout & my cat jumps out
of her basket & runs for the door.
In the morning Danny is back at work,

& I'm crying with relief that he's safe, sober.
But I know it won't last. Like the time my father
ended up in the Heritage Hotel with a shotgun.

I'm afraid to watch next week's episode
& can't wait. Can't wait to remember the time
I snorted lines of coke for eight hours

then got into a hot tub & almost died.
Tonight, I drink a glass of water & go to bed early.
The later it gets, the darker it gets,

I thought when I was a girl.
I would do anything to help Danny, Daddy,
even though it's impossible.

Smart TV

you buy a smart tv   it's so smart
it takes four days to figure out
you finally find the series someone said is good
right away there's a dead woman
on a bridge who's been cut in half at the waist
half of her is in denmark   the other half in sweden   clever
at least she isn't naked   she's smartly dressed
her intestines neatly coiled
under her suit jacket   you get a peek at them
when the police move her to the lab for identification
the upper half is a swedish politician   the lower a danish prostitute
politicians & prostitutes   kind of cliché   you watch a while longer
asking the same dumb question   why are dead women
so interesting   you change the channel & it's law & order
special victims unit   sexual molestation rape kidnapping mutilation
you could watch hallmark   snow angels
cookie baking pillow fighting homophobic white people
you'll stick with dead women   various colors   rising up
women zombie detectives   a special unit   even a wall
won't stop them   can't get rid of them   they're already killed
solving the case once & for all   you turn off the tv
the silence brilliant

Black Friday

we are destroying the world   should I take these shoes back
I could get them stretched   Greenland is melting
where is my shopping list   do I need a coal mine
a clean one   a bigger car with more apps
& custom vinyl wrap   methane is leaking from the seafloors
do I need a mop   the town where my mother grew up
burned down   Paradise California   it was famous
for red dirt   the president called the town Pleasure twice
he said we need safe forests   very safe forests
& that is happening   he said   as we speak
through our n95 masks   as we shop
the Antarctic ice sheet is collapsing   the permafrost is liquefying
pleasure pleasure   que será será
my mother & I sang while driving through the Sierras
so I would get my mind off vomiting   distraction
works   where are you going on vacation   the continents boil
have a nice trip   keep your mouth shut while swimming
plastic plastic   during thanksgiving week so many planes
they had to use military airspace   they us   who is innocent
what happened to our eyes   what does the polar bear see
rhino warbler salmon tiger   the golden toad last seen
in 1989 in the Costa Rican cloud forest   what does the cloud see
the violet the mango the red dirt   we are in peril
the stores are sold out

Flamenco

Because of the smoke, the sun is orange
as I walk around the shrinking lake,
the light casting a turmeric glow on my arms,
on everyone's legs in summer shorts,
on the chest of the shirtless man running
toward me, his shoes untied.

I worry he'll trip, but he seems unconcerned.
He carries an iPhone in one hand,
a stereo speaker in the other,
delivering a dance tune to the scorched air.

We want a song no matter what and heat
between bodies, sweat glittering like broken glass
along a collarbone, someone to flamenco with
at least for a few moments, laces flailing,
the burnt sky burning through us.

A flotilla of mallards glides by,
dipping green heads tinged tangerine
into the greasy water. The future visible
as a clavicle. Under the skin of smoke, lovers
lie on the shore, kissing like wildfire.

Hot as Hell

The planet warmed up,
so we bought an air conditioner.
The AC was LOL but also our BFF
until our last scorched whimper.
This was the era when language shrank
and we grew into hunchbacked creatures,
squinting away from each other into our cell
phones at our FB feed. It was HAH,
so we mostly stayed inside, ordering
hug-me pillows from Amazon.
We were SAD, which meant too many things:
Seasonal Affective Disorder, Seek and Destroy,
Sons and Daughters. BTW, what about them—
our daughters and sons?

Great

My cat's been vomiting. Needs an ultrasound.
"That's a high-ticket item," says the assistant vet,

who hands me a piece of paper with numbers
in long columns. When I read the estimate,

I think my cat is a car. The ultrasound costs $600,
and I should include a cystocentesis, "Because if she has a mass,

we can't identify it unless we do the cysto. And blood work,
along with another ultrasound, because the doctor heard

a faint murmur, don't worry, it was really faint, but we need
to check her heart." "So you're saying," I say, "that I'm paying

$1,392 before you can tell me what's making her sick?"
"That's the low end," the assistant says. "The total's between $1,392

and $1,698 because of miscellaneous." "Miscellaneous," I say. I say,
"What do poor people do when their pet gets sick?" and feel sick

I said it. Not the assistant's fault that if you're poor and your pet
gets sick you let it die like I'll let my cat die if I can't afford

the surgery, even though she's only four years old.
I think of the children who get sick and can't pay to live.

Who can pay to live anymore? The rich, the rich. I want to vomit,
wishing I were rich every expensive American day.

The assistant says maybe I should talk to the doctor. "That'd be great,"
I say, and wait in the little cell of a room, staring at a box of tissues

ready for plucking. I stuff a few in my pocket because I could
cry but don't know what to cry about first. Do you?

What if we all stopped doing anything except wailing
from coast to coast for our bilious country,

our tears flooding the capital, drowning the dancing rats?

Ms. Scrooge

jesus mary sheep & cows okay
but come on with santa & reindeer
especially the blinking red nose
good I guess for kids during the darkest month
one of my favorite gifts was a dildo
at the party my married friends gave it to me
I went home with it   fell asleep
from the champagne   woke up screaming
something moving under the covers
making a sound like a strangled cicada
I jumped   ripped the sheet off
a writhing dildo on its last legs   leg
on new year's eve I bought batteries
embarrassed as if the clerk knew
what they were for   when I put them in
the dildo didn't work   turned the batteries around
but I had a broken dildo on my hands   I could have
gone to the outskirts of town   bought another one
that's where dildos were kept in those days
in the treeless places with the windowless bars
& used tires piled like an american pyramid
behind the chain link
I was an elementary school teacher
what if someone saw me at the sex toy store
the whole thing as agonizing
as christmas   bad attitude I know
blame it on the dildo

Auld Lang Syne

he wants to lose ten pounds   doesn't like his small paunch
most people our age have a small medium
or large paunch   drink less   good idea in theory
more sex   can't argue with that   I once had sex
in a cemetery   not sure why I tell him this
he recalls how once after a wedding he ended up in a cemetery
in a car having sex   I've never had sex in a car
even though it's like valentine's day   he thinks having sex
in a car is a wonderful goal for the year   he's had sex
in a car many times   highly recommends it   this makes me a little jealous
he never had sex in a car with me   maybe the problem was our cars
I didn't have one   he had a patched-up exhausted chevy   we were raw
as the weather   didn't last a season   only a few fast months of darkness
rain tule fog   couldn't get warm enough drink enough beer smoke enough
cigarettes to cure what we didn't know hurt   sex was urgent then
trying to forget the self   find a place to rest so we could survive
our youth   I had opportunities   was it the gearshift knob
cemetery sex seems preferable   flat ground
possibly lawn & flowers   I moved to colorado
the cemetery was in the mountains   we were like tumbleweeds
rolling between the gravestones   I thought of my friend
how he was doing   oh the ghosts of us   another year
to add to the haunting   the new already a week old
life up and goes like having sex in a moving vehicle
my friend & I trying to keep something from the ever-fleeting
he has to get going   so many ways to say goodbye
farewell so long take care godspeed

While Playing Tennis
I Never Think of Death

Instead, I notice the clouds like a white shag rug
when I toss the ball up high for the serve,

my face filling with sky and neon-green fuzz,
and then that wonderful thwack

as I smash matter against matter
with the body's happy violence.

Game over, my opponent leaves for work,
and there's nothing as glorious as an empty

tennis court surrounded by oak trees
on a morning in October.

So why does sadness flow
like bees and honey through my chest,

and I suppose that's too poetic,
but brace yourself for more: tears fall,

and I'm sure you'll groan when I revise
and tell you the little valleys beneath my eyes

are wet, or perhaps I should get literal
and precisely name them—wrinkles.

Don't worry, the seizure of feeling
has passed, and I won't mention autumn

or longing like the breeze lifting
the edges of the clouds and rolling them up

to disappear into infinity's storage unit.
I won't say a thing about the V of geese rising

above the chain-link fence, their calls
sounding exactly like nuns keening,

and not a whisper will I breathe
about my hunger for God.

I will go do my errands and pretend living
doesn't sometimes rip my heart like a backhand shot

down the line, or too often seem like dandelion dust
scattering over the beautiful, mortal tennis court.

Tremolo

a car door hanging open   a young woman
holding her phone   crying
the kind of crying beyond help
but you ask   she shakes her head
you leave her in her sorrow   its violence
shaking her like a rag doll
walk up the stairs to the tree-lined path
join the other walkers celebrating saturday
the moments unfolding like an accordion
under the movement of stars planets one trillion galaxies
in the observable universe   fate working silently
so much happening good & bad
almost lose their meaning   hear her crying
inside you   pray from the heart to the heart
of grief   to the bond between dog dragonfly dahlia
blood salt light   back where you started
another car in that space
shaking   music blasting

In the Wine Country

Sunday, late winter, but warm enough
to have the top down,
and she could almost touch
the Spanish moss draping
the trees in gauzy-green
swaths of torn silks.
They'd been married for years,
and there was no one else
she wanted to spend
this amount of time with,
talking or in silence.
"I like our quiet life," he would say
when she asked if he was sad
they'd never had a child.
Sometimes she thought they were
like orphans, raising each other
in the wild of shared solitude.
They drove all day, stopping
for a glass of wine, a sandwich,
or to walk along a ridge of manzanitas.
She kissed him by the river.
His mouth tasted of merlot
and memories of all their kisses.
She would not recover from him, ever.
The sun dropped behind the hills
as they drove home.
He asked if she wanted to stop;
they could put the top up.
She said, "Let's keep going,"
although her eyes were stinging from the cold,
and the sky was a field of darkness.

Shepherd Canyon

I walk down the path in Shepherd Canyon,
    With my hurt knee and sore hamstring,
Thinking about what never heals, wishing
    I believed in something besides the sun falling
Below the hills, shadow taking over
    Everything, and then I see three people,
Maybe parents and their child.
    The father and son walk side by side,
The mother behind them, and they are softly
    Singing in a language I don't understand.
The father has his hand on the boy's back,
    Steadying his son, the boy is eleven
Or twelve and can't walk very well, his head bobs,
    His tongue hangs out. The father sometimes takes
His son's arm and lifts him upright like they've
    Been doing this dance all the boy's life,
And the mother keeps the song going,
    And when I pass them, they fall silent,
So I walk as fast as pain will let me,
    Not wanting to interrupt them, and after
I'm far enough away, they start singing again,
    And I can barely hear it, but I hear it.

Mandolin Sky

Dark out when he leaves for work now,
& we kiss & wish each other a good day,
& the door shuts, the lock clicks, the sound
of his steps on the gravel fades, & I try to fall back
asleep, pull the covers to my chin
& fold them perfectly, but the angels
come to wrestle with me in a stream
of shifting shapes: My father at the table,
lifting the spoon wrapped with noodles
to his mouth after saying,
I've taught you all I know, you're on your own.
The lover from long ago who waited
in the cold car until I came home
from waitressing smelling of chowder & beer,
how that autumn there was no stopping
our loneliness, yet like rain jeweling
the bare branches,
it was part of the beauty.
My friend whose photograph looks at me from the bookshelf
in my office. I can't throw it away, can't put it in a box
in the basement with the mandolin without strings.
Her head leans toward mine, strands of our hair mixing.
She's wearing a feather necklace, a softness
I can almost touch.
I miss you, I miss you, I miss you, like a song's refrain.
Who is the you, what is the missing?
Sometimes I envy people who look past the shattering
& believe the light in our eyes is god.
Did I see it in the hospital, in my father's eyes
a few days before he died? As if
he were on the other side, walking
three blocks west & over the dunes.
We are on our own & never on our own,
part of the one thing appearing in pieces.
There is sadness like pure water washing us
open. Soft light comes through the window
from the gray field of sky broken into clouds
that are lit from within.

Acknowledgments

Thank you to the editors of the publications in which versions of these poems first appeared:

The American Journal of Poetry: "Dare," "Reprieve"

Atlanta Review: "Critical Thinking"

B O D Y: "Just Living"

California Quarterly: "In the Wine Country"

Catamaran: "Chiaroscuro"

The James Dickey Review: "Adventure," "Auld Lang Syne"

Linebreak: "While Playing Tennis I Never Think of Death" (as "Too Poetic"), "This Friday"

Love's Executive Order: "Taking It for a Spin," "Knife"

Mississippi Review: "A Brief History of My Life"

Mudfish: "'What a Wonderful World'"

New Ohio Review: "Valentine"

Rattle: "Strange Ode"

San Diego Poetry Annual: "Mandolin Sky"

Southern Poetry Review: "Shepherd Canyon"

The Southern Review: "Prayer," "Aubade Ending in Elegy," "Variation on Texts by Vallejo, Donald Justice, and Patrick Phillips," "October Violin"

Superstition Review: "Looking for SoHo in SoHo"

SWWIM: "Faith is a Thing with Running Shoes"

"Auld Lang Syne" was long-listed in the Fish Poetry Prize, Fish Publishing

"Critical Thinking" was a finalist in the Fischer Poetry Prize, Telluride Institute

"Mandolin Sky" was a finalist in the Steve Kowit Poetry Prize, *San Diego Poetry Annual*

Thank you to Zack Rogow for selecting this book for the Catamaran Poetry Prize. Thanks to Catherine Segurson, and everyone at *Catamaran Literary Reader*, for supporting this book.

Thank you to Maggie Smith and Matthew Lippman for specific comments on poems and the book's structure.

Thanks again to Matthew Lippman for his wonderful workshop, in which some of these poems had their start.

Other poems began in Kim Addonizio's always-inspirational workshop. Thank you.

Thank you to my writing group for their dedication, talent, and encouragement: Susan Cohen, Rebecca Foust, Julia B. Levine, Roy Mash, and Jeanne Wagner.

Thank you to dear friends and close readers Karen Toloui and K. Patrick Conner.

Thank you to my sisters Cheryl Rossi and Kerry Schur for their love and support.

To Kenneth Jensen: *a thousand kisses deep.*

Susan Browne is the author of two previous poetry collections: *Buddha's Dogs*, winner of the Four Way Books Intro Prize; and *Zephyr*, winner of Steel Toe Books Editor's Prize. Her poems have appeared in *Ploughshares*, *The Sun*, *Subtropics*, *The Southern Review*, *Rattle*, *New Ohio Review*, *American Life in Poetry*, and *180 More, Extraordinary Poems for Every Day*. She was also a recipient of awards from the Los Angeles Poetry Festival, the River Styx International Poetry Contest and the Provincetown Fine Arts Work Center. She lives in Oakland, California.